Computer-Ease

SELECTING YOUR PERSONAL COMPUTER

by
GORDON MORRELL

A JOHN MUIR PUBLICATION

First Edition November 1983

Printed in the United States of America.

Published by: John Muir Publications
P.O. Box 613
Santa Fe, NM 87504

Illustrated by Deborah Reade

Library of Congress Catalogue No. 83-62229

ISBN 0-912528-34-6

Book trade distributor: W.W. Norton & Co., Inc.
New York

To Family and Friends, Past and Present.
But specially to my wife, Sheila.

CONTENTS

Acknowledgements

John Muir has a special place in my life. When his book, *How To Keep Your Volkswagen Alive,* was first published, I was an obvious candidate to buy it: I was "the Compleat Idiot." From John's book I learned about tools, but I also learned about myself. I learned that I was, in fact, capable of doing many things. From adjusting valves and timing my VW engine to other more worldly pursuits, I grew to trust and have confidence in my ability to create and accomplish.

So I've considered it an honor to be published by John Muir Publications and to work with the people there. Special thanks to Ken Luboff, Richard Polese, Deborah Reade, Lisa Cron, Peter Aschwanden, John Stick, Paul Abrams, Jeanne Flannery and Joan Kafri, each for their part in getting this book from me to you.

I'd also like to thank Dana Newquist and the folks at Computer Plaza in Santa Barbara for all their technical assistance, George Taylor and Jib Ray for help with the first drafts, and Radio Shack and Computerland of Santa Fe for help with the illustrations.

I'm sure I've left out just the person to whom I owe the most and would most like to say "thanks," but since you know who you are, please consider it said.

Computer-Ease

PREFACE

I was at a high school science fair not long ago. Along with the obligatory plant exhibits, worm displays and human body drawings were numerous computer displays—all designed by the students. I waited patiently until the kids were gone, and then I stealthily approached one of the machines. I glanced first over one shoulder, then the other, to be sure no one was watching. As my fingers glided to the keyboard an electronic wave of fear swept through me as I realized I had *no idea* what to do!

Frantically I searched the bulletin board displays for directions, but, alas, none were to be found. Out of desperation I hit the RETURN key and listened with amazement as the machine began whirring and characters appeared magically on the television screen. Eureka, I thought, computers are easy—kids' stuff. But my euphoria evaporated when I realized I had totally shut down the program and had not the vaguest notion how to restart it. Truth be known, I couldn't even find the ON/OFF switch.

Defeated, I pushed back my chair just as another busload of adolescents arrived for their tour of the exhibits. The magic-markered human bodies, the plants subjected to total darkness for three months, the dissected worms and frogs, all took a back seat to the new technology. As I watched in awe, the twelve-year-olds lined up to try their fingers and minds on the peer-designed programs. Their confidence was matched only by my dejection as I sheepishly left the fair.

I am the father of two young children and it has been my hope that I could somehow keep up to date with them; that I could in some way build a bridge across the generation gap. I remember when, at age thirteen, I brought my first set theory homework problem for my parents to solve. I remember them collectively shaking their heads. And I remember how that would be the last time they could help with homework. All this is to say that the times are, indeed, a-changin', and my hour in the science fair reminded me that I had made a vow not to get left too far behind.

And so my quest began. Rationalizing as many ways as I could think of for why I "needed" a personal computer, I started searching for the one to best suit me. The experiences that followed are what this book is all about. I've tried to keep three goals in mind thoughout:

1) To give you enough information to make you an informed, intelligent consumer . . .

2) To save you about three months of work—at a very reasonable price . . .

3) To help make your search a bit less humbling than mine was.

Read on and take heart: if I can learn it, you can too!

1 GETTING STARTED

Since we'll be spending at least a couple of hours together, let me fill you in on what we'll be doing. I have written this book to help you learn (and make some decisions) about buying a computer. You're already reading, so I know you are one of the millions of people interested in owning your own computer.

I'm going to give you some basic information about computers, how they work, and what they can do for you—which should help you make the right choice.

I'm assuming you know very little about this area. For example, do you know the difference between a *bit* and a *byte*? Do you still think a *diskette* is a miniature disco dancer? Is there really any difference between CPU and a CP/M?

Here's a secret: four months before starting this book I hadn't any idea what these words meant either... I was in the same situation you are in now.

First I needed to decide whether or not to buy a computer. Once I decided to do it, I had to figure out which one was best for me. I learned one thing very quickly: you've got to know *why* you need or want a computer. What would you like it to do? People will ask you this question all the time, and the answer will help you in your search.

DO YOU REALLY *NEED* A COMPUTER?

The answer to this question is no. Are you still reading? Here's why I think you don't really need a computer: you haven't had one up to now and you're still alive, right? It wasn't too long ago that computers were only for large companies with lots of room and money. Only recently, with the advent of smaller machines and drastically reduced price tags, have folks like ourselves begun thinking that they needed computers. A better question to ask is:

DO YOU REALLY *WANT* A COMPUTER?

Since you've gotten this far, I think the answer is undoubtedly YES, so we can continue with our story. Just for fun, can you list five reasons why you want a computer?

1. ______________________________

____

2. ______________________________

____

3. ______________________________

____

4. ______________________________

____

5. ______________________________

____

Here are a few I thought of:

1. Computers are lots of fun.

2. They can be (are) very educational.

3. They eat less than most large animals.

4. They can make many aspects of your personal and professional life much more efficient.

5. Having your own computer gives you gloating rights over many of your neighbors.

TAKING THE FIRST STEPS

Now that we've established your desire for a computer, it's time for you to do some legwork. Before reading the next chapter, I recommend that you go to a nearby computer store. You can find one by looking in your Yellow Pages under "Computers," "Computer Stores," or something similar. Plan to spend at least thirty minutes to an hour in the store. Just tell any salesperson that you are "interested in maybe buying a computer." He or she will take it from there. Just remember, now's *not* the time to make any commitments . . . that'll come later. You're really "just looking."

When you've finished, go to your nearby bookstore or library and ask for books about computers so you can read about what you've seen. I don't recommend that you buy another book quite yet—just thumb through a few of them and see what you think. Then check the magazine rack. If the bookstore doesn't have one, go to your local magazine shoppe (drugstore?)

where there might be a good supply, or look in the computer store. Pick up at least one of the monthly computer magazines. A few popular titles to search for are:

Personal Computing
Popular Computing
Creative Computing
Interface Age
Desktop Computing
Byte
COMPUTE!

You'll know them when you see them.

When you get back home, read the magazine—especially the advertisements, as these will give you some ideas about what to say next time you're asked to answer questions about your computer needs.

Please try not to panic. It doesn't have to be terribly difficult and technical next time you go to the store. All you really need is a way to communicate with the salespeople. To this end, the "Speaking Computerese" translating dictionary follows in Chapter 2.

2 SPEAKING COMPUTERESE

A Dictionary

Let's begin with a few words from an advertisement in the local newspaper:

> **Standard Hardware:**
>
> - Z80 CPU with 64K RAM
> - Dual floppy disk drives with 102K bytes storage each
> - 5" CRT
> - Business keyboard with numeric keypad and cursor keys
> - RS-232C Interface
> - IEEE 488 Interface

If you know what all of this means you probably can afford to skip this chapter. But for most of us, Computerese is as foreign as any other new language. With the proliferation of new technology has come a new vocabulary as well. Personally, my English is okay, but my Computerese wasn't, and that got me into some problems at the computer store.

The first step I took when I was trying to decide which computer to buy was to go to a dealer—much as you have just done if you followed the instructions in Chapter One. I hope you were better prepared (and therefore less embarrassed) than I was. But maybe you had a similar experience. This was mine:

Believing I knew exactly what I was looking for (and what I was doing), I strode confidently into one of the five or six local computer sales stores in my area.

"What might you be looking for?" the salesperson asked cheerfully.

"A computer," I answered knowledgeably.

"Then you've come to the right place." We both chuckled at the corny diaglogue and got down to serious business.

"What kind of application are you interested in," she asked.

"Application?" I answered (I was beginning to tread on thin ice here).

"What do you want the computer for?" she replied.

"Well, I'll probably be doing quite a bit of word processing (I'd read that in a magazine) and also some data base management" (same source, but I was on a roll—couldn't quit now).

"Then let me show you one of the newest software packages on the market—you'll love it!"

As we took our seats in front of their latest model personal computer I got the immediate feeling that I was getting in over my head.

"Why don't you go ahead and *boot the disk*," she said while feeding paper into the printer.

Deja Vu! I couldn't find the ON switch—I'd been through this before! And "Boot the Disk?" A new-wave song? Frisbee football? I was in trouble now and wanted to leave as soon as I could.

Instead, I sat through a demonstration which was preceded by a description of the computer's capacities ("it has dual density disk drives, a Z80 microprocessor, 64K of RAM, graphics capabilities, two ports for peripherals," etc., etc.). Not knowing what else to do, I asked, "Can you play games on it? I have a four-year-old child" (she shouldn't get the idea that I wanted to play the games, too). That was the beginning of the end. No longer recognized as a bona fide knowledgeable person, I was preempted by a phone call and took my leave.

As I said before, I hope your experience was better than mine. Maybe by now the salespeople are realizing that many of us who are interested in computers are not familiar with the jargon of the business. If so, great! But my guess is that you might have had some trouble understanding what all the new words meant.

Probably the best way to go about learning how to speak Computerese is by finding out a little more about the computer. Let's imagine that the picture below is the real thing, and that you have just asked to have it described to you. Here's what a helpful salesperson (or interpreter) might say:

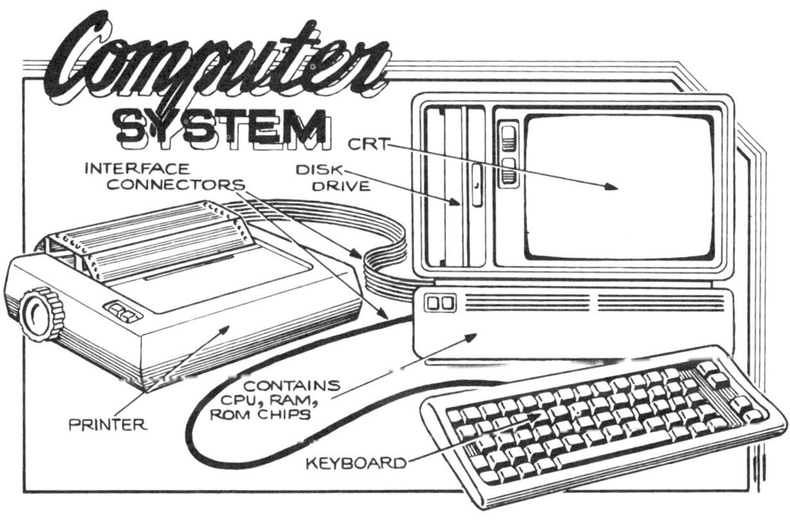

"What you're looking at here is a COMPUTER system. This one has one DISK DRIVE, a MONITOR, and an IMPACT PRINTER. The first thing you might notice is that the COMPUTER looks like an ordinary typewriter. The keyboard is used to INPUT, or enter information, or DATA, into the computer. When you type one CHARACTER, the computer converts it to a BYTE of information. The computer processes your data in its CENTRAL PROCESSING UNIT, or CPU.

"This particular machine has a capacity of 64,000 BYTES, or 64K. Most of this is available as *random access memory*, or RAM. RAM is the part of the computer system that holds information until the computer is ready for it. If you put too much in, the extra is sent out to the DISK, for storage. This can get confusing, so let's turn on the computer and you can see what happens."

(Are you still imagining? Now pretend you can reach into the picture and can turn on the computer. You hear a whirring sound as the salesperson says:)

"Hear that whirring sound? That's the sound of the floppy DISK spinning inside the DISK DRIVE. It is sending information into the CPU of the computer.

"The information at the beginning of the disk is written in CP/M, which is an OPERATING SYSTEM that tells the computer what to do first. The actual PROGRAM is nothing more than a list of instructions for the computer to carry out. You can make up programs yourself, if you want to. This computer will work in BASIC, and that's a fairly easy computer language to learn.

"After you have finished your program, you might want to have a HARD COPY made. The computer uses an INTERFACE to give instructions to the PRINTER. You give the computer a few simple COMMANDS, and it will have the printer show you what it has done. This is really convenient because the only other way to see your work is to have it displayed on the MONITOR, also called CRT.

"Maybe that's enough for now. I have a wonderful book here called *Computer-Ease*. Why don't you take it home with you and read it through? Pay particular attention to the dictionary part—it'll help you understand some of the terms we just talked about."

(You gleefully accept the book—at a very reasonable price, of course—and begin looking through the dictionary. This is what you find:)

THE COMPUTERESE DICTIONARY

NOTE: Words in italics are also defined in the dictionary.

ALPHANUMERIC. Any character which is either a letter (alpha-) or a number (-numeric). What else is there? Don't forget those "special characters" such as !, ", #, $, %, and the ever popular &.

ASCII. Stands for American Standard Code for Information Interchange. ASCII ("as-key") is the computer's way of changing the characters you type into a code it can work with.

BASIC. You will see this on almost every advertisement or book written about computers. BASIC is the Beginner's All-purpose Symbolic Instruction Code. Just as we have a hard time understanding other languages, so does the computer. BASIC is a way of telling the computer what to do since it won't understand just any language. BASIC is a *programming language* which is easier for beginners to follow than other languages such as FORTRAN, COBOL, PASCAL, etc.

BIT. Short for BInary digiT, which is the smallest unit of information a computer can understand. You only need to know this because when you group them together, they become *bytes*, and you will hear alot about bytes. Here's something you'll probably never need to know: there are usually four bits to a nybble, and two nybbles to a byte!

BOOTING THE DISK. To "boot the disk" means to get the computer up and running with whichever *disk* you want in the *disk drive*. When the disk is booted, the control program, or *op-*

erating system, is loaded into the computer's *memory*, thus giving the computer its processing instructions. In a way, this is how the computer begins its conversation with you. From here, the operating system will load other *programs* you wish to run.

BUS. A large motor vehicle generally used for transporting people. Also, a group of wires or pins which carry information to and from the *CPU*.

BYTE. See the bit about bits, above. A byte is roughly equivalent to a *character* (a letter, number, or even a space). Most *disk drives* will be able to store at least 90,000 bytes. To get some sense of how many that is, this definition uses about 260 bytes.

CARD. Depending on your application, you may need one or more of these. A card is a small rectangle of plastic (a little like a playing card) with lots of little circuits and wires on it. These can be used to increase your memory size, add speech capability, or any number of other changes.

CHARACTER. A character is any number, letter, sign, or space. It usually takes eight bits, or one byte of space in the computer.

CHIP. This is the tiny, ubiquitous silicon chip we've all heard so much about. It is the heart and soul of the computer, composed of microscopic circuits which allow the computer to do what it does.

COLUMNS AND ROWS. It's very important to know how much information your computer and *monitor* can display. This is usually measured in columns and rows. A column is the width of one character or space. There may be as many as 80 of these on the monitor screen. Rows are the lines of characters. You might have 25 rows from top to bottom. The size of the display (columns and rows) you need depends on what you will be using your computer for.

COMMAND. You don't have to be polite to your computer—you can command it to do things. Commands are usually words, letters, or phrases that give direct instructions to the computer.

COMPUTER. Finally, we can talk about what a computer is. An official definition is that a computer is something which can accept information (input), remember it (*memory*), do something with the information (process), and show you what it has done (output). If you have all the *peripherals* (we'll get to this one soon) to allow this to happen, you have a computer system. One way to think about a computer is to see it as a list processor. *Programs* are lists of instructions which the computer processes.

CP/M. This stands for Control Program for *Microcomputers*. It is an *operating system* that is supplied with many computers and is said to be the industry standard. A multitude of *programs* are being written under CP/M. When we talk about types of computers to buy, we'll discuss this in more detail.

CPU. This is what most of us refer to as the "computer." CPU stands for Central Processing Unit. Its job is to process information as well as to move it to and from *memory*. The CPU is justifiably called the brains of the computer.

CRT MONITOR. All television sets have a cathode ray tube, or CRT. The *monitors* or video screens used to display input and output for the computer are often referred to as CRTs.

CURSOR. This is usually a little white square that blinks at you to tell you where the next *character* will appear on your *monitor*. Being able to move the cursor (also called "cursor control") easily allows you to enter characters anywhere on the screen. This is extremely important for those who will be inputting lots of *data*.

DAISY WHEEL. One of the questions you will undoubtedly be asked at the store is, "Are you interested in a daisy wheel printer?" A daisy wheel is an *impact printer* (where

letters are put on the paper by keys striking a ribbon) whose typing element looks like a daisy flower. These printers can create "letter quality" copy, like a typewriter.

DATA. This is simply another word for "information," but it is used constantly when discussing computers. You will make yourself look very wise if you remember that data is plural—as in "The data *are* entered into the CPU through the keyboard."

DATA BASE MANAGEMENT. This is a popular *software program* which allows information to be stored in file form. It is the computer version of a file clerk, in that it can manipulate large amounts of data in file form. The *software*, which can cost up to hundreds of dollars, allows you to create files, add information, delete information, search through the files, etc.

DISK (or DISKETTE). This is where your information (data) is stored when it is not in the *memory* of the computer. The disk resembles a small (usually 5.25" or 8.25" diameter) phonograph record. It is made either from metal (rigid, or "hard" disk) or a flexible plastic (hence, "floppy" disk). It uses a magnetic system for its storage medium, and therefore sees any magnet as Diskette Enemy #1.

DISK DRIVE. A *peripheral* device which rotates the disk very quickly so that the computer can retrieve the information on the disk. An entire disk can be searched in seconds. All disk drives have their own *disk operating systems*, or DOS.

Like *CP/M*, DOS is located on the diskette and is read into the computer when you *boot the disk*.

Instead of disk drives, some people buy cassette tape recorders for storage. Unlike disk drives, which can retrieve data from any part of the disk almost instantly, cassette recorders may have to search through the entire tape until it finds the information you need, and that takes time.

DOCUMENTATION. Whenever you purchase a computer, *peripheral*, or even a *software program*, you will undoubtedly receive a few manuals or guides to read. These manuals are referred to as the "documentation" for your purchase.

DOT MATRIX. A way of displaying characters. A dot matrix printer creates letters with a pattern of dots. It's easier to see one at the computer store than to describe it here. But if you've ever seen the time and temperature flashing on one of those lighted signs next to the bank, you know what a dot matrix looks like. Dot matrix isn't as clear as *daisy wheel*, and might not be suitable for business letters.

DOUBLE DENSITY. This is a term which means the capacity of the *disk* has been doubled. Similarly, the term "quad density" tells you that the storage capacity is four times the usual single density.

FORMAT. You'll hear this word quite often when discussing programs and programming. When you "format" the disk, for example, the computer tells the floppy disk where it wants to put information. This format then allows the computer to read and write data on the disk.

FRICTION FEED. This is the ability of some *printers* to send paper through the roller using only friction—no sprockets. This is the same setup used in most conventional typewriters. (See *tractor feed* for a comparison).

GRAPHICS. These are illustrations which are generated by the computer. Graphs, charts and other nonverbal or non-numerical *data* are considered to be graphic representations. Some machines can do these well, others can't. If your applications require use of graphics, be sure the computer you select has good graphics capability.

HARD COPY. Simply a paper display (or "printout") of what the computer has done for you. Without a hard copy, you can review your work only by looking at it on your *CRT*.

HARDWARE. All the physical pieces of your computer system, including what's inside of them, are referred to as hardware. For example, the *CPU, CRT, disk drives* and *printer*, plus all their innards, are hardware. The disks and programs are *software*.

IEEE-488. IEEE is short for the Institute of Electrical and Electronic Engineers. The IEEE-488 is a *parallel interface* used for attaching communications equipment (printers, etc.) to the computer. (See *RS-232C, parallel interface, serial interface* and *interface*.)

IMPACT PRINTER. Any *printer* which makes an image on the paper by striking through a ribbon. *Dot matrix* and *daisy wheel* printers both work this way. Although these are the most popular, you might also come across two other types of printers. The first is the non-impact or thermal printer, which prints by heating specially treated paper. The other is the electrostatic printer, which uses special silvery-colored paper. The need for special papers is the major drawback of the thermal and electrostatic printers.

INTERFACE. This is one term you'll have to use sooner or later, so pay attention. The interface is the device used to connect the computer with the rest of the world. For example, the printer needs to be interfaced with the computer, as do you. Another way to think about this is to imagine yourself in another country where you do not speak the native

language. An interpreter can be thought of as the "interface" between you and the locals. Right now, the industry standard interfaces are the *IEEE-488* and the *RS-232C*. Even if you don't need them now, these may be helpful later on if you want to expand your system.

I/O. This stands for Input/Output and has to do with the communications links between the computer and the outside world. The I/O *port* is located somewhere on the computer terminal. This is where the *printer, disk drive*, or *modem* gets plugged in (see *BUS*).

K. In metric measurement, K stands for kilo, or thousand. In Computerese, K usually means kilobyte, or roughly one thousand *bytes*. More precisely, 1K equals 1,024 bytes, but everyone I know rounds it off to 1,000. So, 48K of *RAM* means the computer can store 48,000 bytes of information in its random access memory.

LANGUAGE. Like us, the computer needs a way to communicate with its users. Different programming languages are available for this purpose, including BASIC, COBOL, FORTH, PASCAL, and many others. If you plan to write your own *programs*, language will be an important factor.

LETTER QUALITY. As in, "Would you like a letter quality printer?" Letter quality means something akin to the type of an IBM Selectric (or similar) typewriter. It's clear and clean. Personally, I use a *dot matrix* printer, and I've sent out letters on it, and I'm even using one for the manuscript of this book. You make the choice, but reread the definitions of *impact printer*, *daisy wheel* and *dot matrix*.

LOADING. Most of the programs or data you will be using are located outside the computer (see *computer*, *memory*, and *interface*). The programs are stored on the disk or tape until needed by the computer. When the computer is ready to use the program, it is transferred, or loaded, from the storage unit into the computer.

MEMORY. This is the storage area, much like that in your own brain. There are two places where information is stored: in the computer and on the disk or tape. When you type a long text, much as I am doing here, all the characters in the text are stored first in the computer's memory, then transferred to the disk. Disk storage is extremely important, because when you shut off the power, all the computer's internal memory is lost. You'll still have whatever you've saved on the disk.

MICROCOMPUTER. This is probably what you will wind up purchasing. The term "micro" means "very small." In the technical sense, all personal computers are very small. There are also other kinds of computers called mini-computers and main-frame computers, but we will not be discussing those here since they are for larger applications.

MICROPROCESSOR. This is the *CPU* of any microcomputer system.

MODEM. Again, this is a term you'll need to know when you go shopping. A modem is something that allows you to hook your computer up to a telephone line. There are services such as The Source, or Dow Jones News/Retrieval which allow microcomputer users to get input (see *I/O*) from those central services by using a modem.

MONITOR. Without one of these your computer is not going to be very useful. The monitor allows you to see what you and your computer are doing. Generally the monitor is a *CRT* or an ordinary TV set. As the technology improves, we will be seeing more monitors made with LCD displays (such as digital wristwatches have) that are virtually paper-thin. Be aware that monitors made specifically for computers will give you a sharper picture than your TV can.

NUMERIC PAD. This is not a place to live that has a lot of numbers in it. A numeric pad is a set of typing keys (usually 0 through 9, +, −, ×, ÷, and return key) set off to the right side of the regular keyboard. These keys are set up like a hand calculator and allow rapid entry of numbers. Some computers which do not have built-in numeric pads may have them installed as *peripherals*.

OPERATING SYSTEM. The computer needs an operating system to run, as does the *disk drive*. The operating system is the *software program* which controls the overall operations of the system. It is like a mediator which runs between the *hardware* and the program instructions. *CP/M* is an operating system which runs some computers, but there are many others. Your choice of a computer may be based on which operating system the software you need is written for.

PARALLEL INTERFACE. A parallel interface (like the IEEE-488) transmits data one *byte* at a time. While this is faster than serial transmission, it is also more expensive, more complicated to design, and causes more interference with household appliances. Nonetheless, the IEEE-488 is becoming more popular and is worth having as an *I/O port*.

PERIPHERAL. The *disk drive* or cassette recorder, the *monitor*, the *printer*, and the *modem* are all peripherals. That is, they are extra devices that are connected to and controlled by the computer.

PERSONAL COMPUTER. These are what this book is written about. A personal computer is a small (by technical standards), low-cost (compared to minis and mainframes) *microcomputer*. I'll discuss different kinds of personal computers in Chapter Five.

PIXEL. This cute-sounding word is a contraction meaning "PICture ELement." Each pixel is like an individual point of light which can be turned on or off. The more pixels you have, the greater will be your ability to do very detailed graphics.

PORT. Besides being a wine of dubious distinction, the port is the external part of the computer's inside wiring. You will plug your *peripherals* into a port.

PRINTER. The device which gives you a hard (paper) copy. It takes information from the computer and puts it on paper. Printers come in a variety of sizes, prices and features. Some can give you full color, others can give you letter quality. It's very important to be sure you have a printer that can do what you need!

PROGRAM. This is a list of instructions that you or someone else can write in order to tell the computer what to do. Remember that you will need to understand another *language* to do this, such as BASIC, FORTRAN, or whatever language is built into the computer. For those of us who don't know about writing our own programs, there are literally thousands of them on the market which we can buy and plug in to our systems. There are programs to play games, programs to write checks, do personal budgeting, run full-scale bookkeeping systems, etc.

RAM. This is one of the favorite buzzwords of the computer industry. You'll do well to learn the difference between RAM and *ROM*. RAM stands for Random Access Memory. The RAM capacity comes with the computer, but the information can be programmed and retrieved easily. When a program is loaded into the computer's *memory* from the disk or tape, it goes into the RAM. When you shut the power off, anything in RAM is forever lost.

RF MODULATOR. A device which allows an ordinary household TV to be used as a *monitor*. Particularly useful for playing games in full color, the RF modulator simply hooks up between the computer and the antenna screws on the TV.

ROM. Like *RAM*, ROM is a type of *memory*. It means Read Only Memory. Literally, you can only read what is available in ROM; you cannot reprogram it. This information is written to give instructions to the computer when you turn it on. The computer manufacturer does the programming before you buy the computer, and builds it in so that it is always there for the computer to read. It stays there even after the power is shut off. When you turn the computer on again, ROM is ready to go.

RS-232C. Like the *IEEE-488*, it is one of the standard *interfaces*. The difference is that the RS-232C is a *serial interface*.

SCROLLING. Obviously your *monitor* can only show you so much information at one time. Right now, for example, I can only see about twenty lines of type on my monitor as I write this, but I know there are pages more of text behind those lines. Scrolling is the ability to move text from off-screen to on-screen, by one or more lines or columns at a time.

SERIAL INTERFACE. This type of *interface* (the *RS-232C*, for example) transmits data *bit* by *bit*. Therefore, it is slower than the *parallel interfaces*. The RS-232C is commonly used, however, and should be a factor in your decision making.

SOFTWARE. Although not really "soft," software refers to *programs* which run the computer. The term distinguishes the programs from *hardware*, or the actual mechanical and electrical components of the machine.

TRACTOR FEED. Like *friction feed*, this refers to the way in which the paper goes through the printer. A tractor feed system uses sprockets (spikes) which engage small holes in the paper. The sprockets turn on rollers and pull the paper along, out of the paper box and through the printer. Unless your work is going to be mainly single sheet, tractor feed is a good thing to have. A big advantage of tractor feed is that it assures accurate, reliable paper feed. *Friction feed* printers can use roll or continuous-feed paper too, but the paper tends to move around on the carriage of the printer.

WORD PROCESSING. Word processing *software* allows you to do things with words. You can write, edit on the screen, reformat, move whole sentences or paragraphs around, print the text on the printer, etc. Word processing is available on software at almost any computer store for all but the smallest machines.

* * * * *

That should be enough to get you started. If you are a real linguist, or glutton, you can buy a more elaborate computer dictionary at your favorite bookstore. Naturally, these go into much more detail than I have done here.

In case you're wondering what value all these words will have in your new vocabulary, keep in mind that many of them have no English counterpart. (For example, RAM is *RAM* and ROM is *ROM*.) You have to know what these words mean because, for one thing, the salespeople will keep using them.

3 HARDWARE

There's a hardware store a few blocks from here where the floors are made of old oak boards and where the nuts and bolts are still kept in big bins instead of plastic bags. Further down the street is another hardware store where the nuts and bolts are called "integrated circuits" and the hardware is computers, printers, disk drives, and other peripherals. I imagine that the old-fashioned hardware stores, like the corner grocery, will always be around. But I think the new hardware is here to stay, too. Now it's time for us to try to understand what this new hardware is all about.

THE COMPUTER

Let's start with an analogy. Picture yourself trying to make an important decision. For example, suppose you are trying to decide whether or not you want to buy a computer. You start by collecting lots of information. To this you add ideas you've had stored in your mind recently and in the past. Then you might sit down with paper and pencil and list all the pros and cons regarding your decision. Finally, the decision made, you act on it. Now turn back a few pages and re-read our Computerese

Dictionary definition for *computer*.

In our analogy, your brain does what a computer does: takes in information, processes it, remembers it, and shows you what has happened. Of course, there is a major difference. Computers are not able to "think" for themselves quite the way you can. They can only do what they are told—what they are programmed or instructed to do. (One advantage to this system is that if the computer has a failure in one of its circuits, that circuit can be found and replaced. It's a bit more complicated with a brain.) But the great similarity between the brain and the computer lies in what they both have to do. You can check your local library for a book on how the brain works. Here we're going to spend the next few pages looking at how the computer goes about its business.

INPUT

You probably already know how information gets into the computer. Almost without exception, the personal computer user will enter information (program and data) through a typewriter-style keyboard. The day will come, to be sure, when voice transmission will replace this method, but for now the keyboard seems to be the norm.

Keyboards come in two main types: membrane and mechanical. The membrane keyboard is a flat piece of plastic on

which are printed letters, numbers and symbols. You touch the plastic membrane to enter the character. While fine for game playing and mopping off spilled cola, the membrane keyboard isn't the best for serious computing. You can't feel keys beneath your fingers.

The mechanical keyboard looks exactly like that of a regular typewriter. However, not all of them are alike. Each machine has a slightly different feel, and some of the characters may be in different locations. You must try out the keyboards to find which one you like using. Also take note that some keyboards only have numbers along the top row (like a standard typewriter), while others have separate number keys (numeric pads) designed like the numbers on a hand calculator. If you will be using lots of numbers, this factor might take place in your decision-making.

PROCESSOR

Something has to happen to the information after you enter (input) it. As with the brain, the computer has to process the data or instructions given to it. The processor (called "microprocessor" in personal computers) is usually a silicon *chip* containing thousands of electronic circuits. These are like microscopic fence gates which open and close electronically, and almost magically allow the computer to understand what you've told it.

Because of what it looks like and what it does, the microprocessor is sometimes called a *microchip* or the *CPU* (Central Processing Unit). While you don't need to know much more about microprocessors, be aware that there are many different types on the market. You should ask questions about the one you are about to purchase. The two most widely used chips are the 6502 (in the Apple, Atari, Commodore, Mattel, and others) and the Z80 (used in the TRS-80, Xerox, Osborne, North Star, Hewlett Packard, etc.). What's the difference? For most of us, any differences will not be significant, with one major exception: only the Z80 microprocessor and its close relatives can use CP/M software. Even this statement will be obsolete soon, as new chips are created to act like the others. For example the Apple computer, which has the 6502, can operate CP/M programs if you install an accessory card containing the Z80 processor. It's confusing, but this is not the place to worry! Choosing between microprocessors probably won't be the point on which your decision about buying a computer is based.

Now, what good is all this if the computer doesn't know what to do? Remember, despite what you may have heard, the computer is not an entirely intelligent being. It needs instructions, which must be supplied by thinkers (usually people). These instructions are stored in the computer's *memory*—the subject of our next discussion.

MEMORY

Remember the definitions of ROM and RAM in our Computerese Dictionary? Let's review. ROM is the Read Only Memory. It was programmed into the computer at the factory and it's there permanently—you can't change it. The purpose of ROM is to give instructions to the computer beginning as soon as it is turned on. Some elementary procedures can be run on this built-in program, but for major applications you will be using the RAM, the Random Access Memory. This information is obtained at random by the computer. It doesn't live inside the machine the way ROM does. Usually the RAM data is stored on a tape or

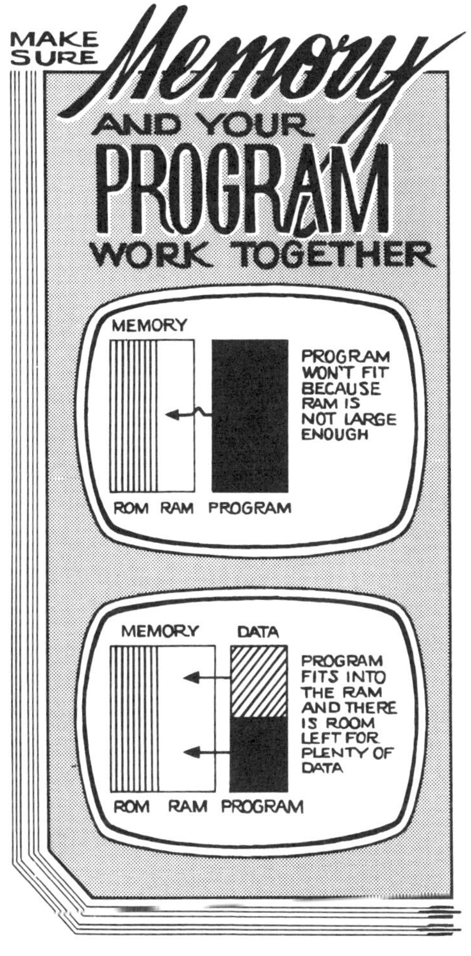

disk drive and is entered into the computer memory when you need it.

If you still have trouble figuring out the difference, consider this: ROM is like a book and RAM is like a chalkboard. RAM you can erase or change as needed, and ROM is always there—even after you've finished for the day.

What's really important about ROM and RAM is that every computer advertisement and every salesperson will mention them, so you need to understand what they are. Also, you should know that the size of your programs will be limited by the amount of memory your computer can hold. For example, if you are buying a computer for the sole purpose of running games, educational programs, or household budgets, 4K to 8K (remember: "kilobytes") of memory will be sufficient. For serious programming and for many off-the-shelf programs, 16K to 32K is required. When you get into business applications, particularly CP/M programs, you will almost always need 48K to 64K of memory. Be sure to ask how much of that is in ROM (built-in) and how much is really available for your programs.

Here's a rule of thumb to use: for home applications such as games, budgets, checkbooks, recipes, etc., the more ROM you have (12K-24K), the easier your job will be. For more complicated applications and programs, the ROM can take up valuable space needed for RAM. In these cases, less ROM (12K and under) will be more efficient.

STORAGE

Let's assume you are looking at a computer that has a memory of 48K. While this might be fine for writing programs and storing some data, it gets filled up very quickly when you start adding more information. You need another place where the information can be stored and retrieved quickly. This "extra" information can be put on either a cassette tape or a floppy disk. As needed, the computer can go out and get this information from the tape or disk. For example, right now I have a word processor program loaded into the RAM of my computer. The program tells the computer what to do with the characters I type. As I type more characters than the RAM in the computer can hold, they are sent out to be stored on my disk drive. If I need to read those words later, the computer will retrieve them for me.

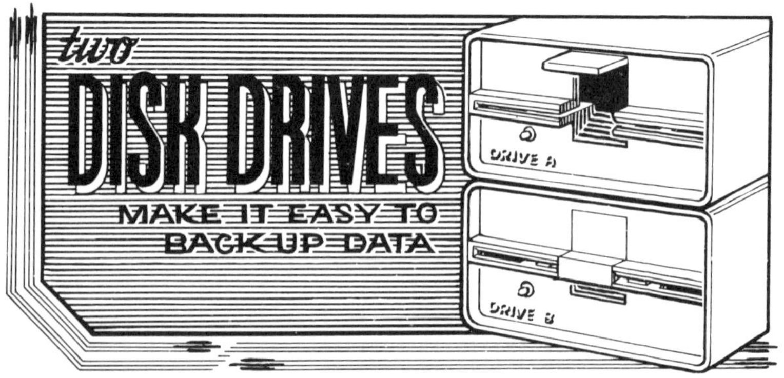

The major difference between cassette storage systems and disks is *speed*. If I had put my text on a 30-minute tape, and needed to read something I had written in Chapter Two, it could take up to half an hour for the tape to wind through the cassette as the computer searches for the information. With a disk drive the same task takes about one second.

For all but the most basic applications (such as video games), a disk drive is worth the initial extra expense (about \$350 more than a cassette tape player). The disk drives you will be looking at will probably use *floppy disks*—so named because they are rather flexible. These are usually 5.25" (but sometimes 8.25") in diameter and will hold in excess of 90,000 bytes. With double density, dual-sided disks, storage capacity increases to 360K per disk drive.

If you really have masses of information to store, you might consider a *hard disk system*. The hard disk is a rigid (as opposed to floppy) device which generally is not removable from the drive. The advantage to the hard disk is that it can store up to 5 *megabytes* (that's 5,000,000 bytes!) on a five-inch disk, or up to 12 megabytes (!) on an eight-inch system. A big disadvantage is that hard disk systems cost more, up to nine times the cost of a comparable floppy disk drive in some cases.

In either case, the drive itself works like a phonograph player. Instead of using a needle to "read" the grooves, the disk drive has a magnetic head that reads and writes on the disk with magnetic pulses.

As with the microprocessor, you don't have to understand all the mechanics of the storage system in order to use it. Again, become familiar with the basics so that you can get the information you need when you go to the computer store.

OUTPUT

Imagine owning a computer and not being able to see what you've done with it. Having only the hardware we've discussed so far, you would have no means of reviewing your work. The keyboard sends information into the computer, the disk or cassette machine stores it, the CPU processes, but you can't see what is going on. (If you type the way I do, this can be a real problem.) But read on . . .

Monitor (CRT)

No computer system is complete without some form of output—usually a video monitor (CRT). These look like ordinary TV sets and, indeed, some computer applications are well suited for use with the TV set in your home. For example, if your sole purpose in buying a computer is to play the wildly popular arcade-type games, connecting the computer to your TV will be just fine. You can attach a simple device called an *RF modulator* in very little time. For more complex applications, however, you will want a monitor made specifically for the computer. These will give you a much clearer picture. Moreover, with a separate monitor you won't have to compete for TV time with the rest of your family.

Video display monitors come in either one color (green, or amber, or black letters on a white screen) or in full color. The single-color (you might hear them called *monochrome*) screens are usually better for projects needing greater detail (high resolution) such as word processing, data base management, etc. For graphic displays, sophisticated video games and other color needs, a full-color monitor is the only option.

As with everything else in your decision-making process, you need to know your present applications and have some idea of your future needs. Word processing, for example, requires a system that will display all the information you write. Displays of less than 80 characters across (the standard for an 8 1/2-inch paper width) can be difficult because you can't see the entire line, as it will be printed, all at once. Some brilliant software writers are already producing programs which will display characters graphically in excess of the machine's capacity. Ask about these when you go shopping.

Printers

Personally, my own powers of memory and recall can't quite compare to that of my computer, so I like to have a "hard copy" to look at. This is where the printer comes in. Information can be sent out to the video screen, or the printer, or to both at the same time.

While there are as many printers on the market as there are personal computers, almost all of those designed for home and business use are *impact printers* (back to the Computerese Dictionary) and they fall into two major categories: *dot matrix* and *formed character*. The dot matrix printer makes characters by printing a pattern of dots on the paper. The formed character printers work by pressing the whole character image through a ribbon onto the paper. These are usually called *letter quality* printers, because they produce sharp, clear characters, much like those of an electric typewriter. All impact printers are relatively noisy, very fast, and can use ordinary paper. Most of today's printers allow you to use either fan-fold paper (the kind that fits over sprockets and gets pulled into the printer) or individual sheets of paper (if the printer has *friction feed*).

In the non-impact category, the most popular printers operate by electronically burning characters into specially treated paper. For this reason they're called "thermal" printers. While they are much quieter and generally less expensive than the impact printers, thermal printers require special types of paper, which will add to your costs. And these papers cannot give the same appearance of typewritten quality the way an impact printer can, so your copies might be of limited value.

Like automobiles, all printers do basically the same thing, but vary tremendously in their options and quality. Spend a good deal of time having printers demonstrated before you buy one. Be sure it can do what you need!

INTERFACES

Talking about interfaces is more difficult than other parts of the system, because you can't really see them. The interfaces are installed within the inner sanctums of the machinery. An interface allows the computer to communicate with its peripherals—the disk drives, printers, modems, etc. One catch with some interfaces is that they can only be used with peripherals manufactured by the same company. This is something you should find out about when you shop for your system. Beyond that, the function of the interfaces should not be of great concern in your decision-making—just know that they're there.

HOME IS WHERE MY COMPUTER IS

We can't end our discussion of computer hardware without talking about the space it is about to occupy. This will generally be a home or office environment, and in either case you need to be careful that your new family or office member will be happy in its surroundings.

Let me tell you a true story:

I live in a "cute and cozy" house—so the real estate agent said. There is enough room for Sheila and me, our two children, two of our own cats and a few strays, but that's about all. On computer purchase day, I arrived at the front door with three large cartons (the computer, monitor and printer) two smaller ones (disk drives), a box of fan-fold paper, and a bag full of software, instruction booklets, and other assorted necessities. These were transported, one at a time and gingerly, to our upstairs bedroom, which also contains my desk—the ultimate destination of this journey. Each piece was carefully unpacked and assigned a space on the desk. I found out two things at this point: there was no way to feed the paper into the printer, and there wasn't enough room on my desk top for all the equipment anyway.

There's a lesson in this for you. Please take the time to *measure* your work area before you try setting up your system. I wound up having to move everything back downstairs—into the garage, which was my only other option. Fortunately, we don't live in a place where we have to put the family car in with the family computer, so this didn't work out too badly. But I had to buy tables, filing cabinets and other office equipment which added to my overall cost. Buyer—beware!

Besides measuring, you need to think about a few other things before you set up your system. Here are some things your computer will not like:

1. Excessive heat.

2. Excessive humidity (keep away from laundry rooms and Washington, D.C. in the summer).

3. Peanut butter and jelly (small children could present problems.)

4. Any liquid refreshment poured into the keyboard.

5. Magnets. Keep these away from your computer and your disks at all costs! Magnets or magnetic fields will destroy hours of your work and/or purchased software instantly.

And here are some things you need to consider:

1. Your application. As we have discussed throughout this book, application dictates almost everything else. If your sole computer use is for games, you'll probably want to set it up in the TV room. If you will be doing more serious work, such as word processing or business use, try to have a quiet, well-lighted area.

2. You will always need room for papers and manuals. Have enough tabletop or desktop space to accomodate your computer, disk drives, printer, CRT, and office paraphernalia, plus open space to lay out the reading material.

3. Have room available for a bookshelf and a filing cabinet. Believe it or not, you still will collect quite a bit of paper, even though you have information stored on disk. Most people don't feel comfortable unless they can touch that important data. The bookshelf will come in handy as you collect magazines and books which help you understand the computer world.

4. Plan on using at least *three outlets* to plug in your system. While they need not be on a separate circuit, it is a good idea to keep them free of any circuit which carries a large electrical load. Refrigerators and washing machines

tend to pull extra juice from the line as their motors go on and off. This might affect data in your RAM.

5. Your electrical outlets should be of the 3-pronged type. This will ground your system and prevent electrical shock. It will also reduce interference with radios and TVs in your home or office. You should discuss this with an electrician, but it is probably not a good idea to change the plugs to match the outlets. It is better to change the outlets.

6. If you are planning to use a modem (see the Computerese Dictionary), be sure you can get a telephone line located near the computer. A quick check with the phone company might help you decide on your workspace location.

7. Finally, just plain olde common sense should help you plan your environment. Think about your present and future uses and remember my story. Planning ahead is the name of the game when deciding where your computer is going to go.

This may be redundant, but the message cannot be overstated: the most important thing about buying and locating a system is knowing what you want it to do. Whether it's playing games, doing advanced level scientific programming or writing books, identifying your needs is the first step in deciding what to get and where to put it.

All the information given here about hardware will help you understand the systems you examine—but only you can determine which one will be best. We will explore that in more detail in Chapter Six. Meanwhile, now that we have the hardware under control, let's see what can be done with it. We'll be talking about *software*.

4 SOFTWARE

Having a computer system without software would be like having a car without gas, or like being all dressed up with no place to go. Software is a term for the programs which tell the hardware how to operate. We will introduce four types of software here: the Disk Operating System (DOS), write-your-own, hire-someone-else-to-write-it-for-you, and off-the-shelf programs.

Keep in mind that there is a vast variety of software out there—so choose carefully.

"DOS" PROGRAMS

The DOS is common to any disk drive system, although each manufacturer's DOS will differ slightly from all the others. Its job is to transfer information from the disk to the computer and vice versa. When you turn on the computer you "boot the disk," meaning you get the Disk Operating System working and the program loaded. Once the disk is booted the computer can get its directions from the DOS, and you can go ahead and enter your own instructions on the keyboard. The DOS will take care of most of the nitty-gritty chores that keep the computer operating smoothly.

WRITE-YOUR-OWN PROGRAMS

If you believe that the only way to get a job done right is to do it yourself, the computer allows you this option. Of course, you will have to learn about programming in the computer's native language, but there is no reason why you can't write a program to run on your machine. Programs are nothing more than lists of instructions that tell the computer what to do.

You've heard that old adage: "Computers don't make mistakes—people do." Mostly true. Computers generally only do what they are told to do. When you write a program, you give the computer a list of things to do in order to perform a certain task. The computer is programmed by typing instructions on the keyboard into the computer's memory. Once you finish the program it can be saved on a disk and used over and over again.

HIRE-SOMEONE-ELSE-TO-DO-IT

The great advantage to writing your own is that you get exactly what you want—no more, no less. Plus, since you wrote the program, you know its exact capabilities and limitations. Another major advantage is the cost factor. Besides your time, your program will probably cost you about $4.00—the cost of a single floppy disk.

If you are like me, however, the cost would be much higher, since you would have to add in the price of coffee to stay awake at night until the programming was done, plus the cost of aspirin to stave off the headaches. Realizing all this in advance, it might be worth your while to hire someone to write the software for you, particularly if you have a complex problem requiring skill and experience. Programmers abound, but you should get references much as you would for the family dentist. You will invest a lot of time and money if you choose this route, so you'll want to get it done well.

OFF-THE-SHELF SOFTWARE

Last and most, there is the pre-packaged, off-the-shelf, highly advertised commercial software. For an indication of how this business has grown, you should consult the annual *Software Buyer's Guide*, published by *Creative Computing* magazine. The most recent edition listed more than 500 companies in its Directory of Software Manufacturers. The advertisements alone will give you literally hundreds of programs to choose from. Remember, though, to find out what you're buying before you commit your hard-earned dollars. Software advertisements are designed to sell the program, not necessarily to define and fill your needs. Be sure you are getting what you need. If you know someone who has a computer, see if she or he has tried the software you have in mind. Does it really do what it is supposed to do? Have there been any problems? Does the manufacturer support (offer assistance for) the program?

To give you an example of this last point, I bought a word processing program to help me write this book. I misread one of the instructions and inadvertently ruined part of the program. I returned the diskette to the manufacturer with a brief letter of explanation and *voila!*—three days later a new diskette arrived in the mail. It's reassuring to know this kind of service is available, and I would recommend that company's software to anyone who asks.

DOCUMENTATION

Related to the question of manufacturer's support is the area know as documentation. This refers to the books or manuals which generally accompany the software. They are supposed to tell you how to use the program. Fortunately, most manuals are written for people like you and me. But some assume an advanced knowledge of Computerese, including some programming ability! It's a good idea to browse through the software manuals before you buy to be sure you'll understand how it works when you get it home. This is an advantage to buying through a store as opposed to through the mail. Unless the mail-order outlet has a money-back guarantee, you could wind up with an expensive program that you can't figure out how to use.

SOFTWARE CATEGORIES

To discuss all the different types of software available to you would be impossible, but we can look at some of the major categories under which software is sold.

Word Processing

These are programs which allow you to do things with words. You can create text, edit it, move it around, add to it, delete it, etc., all without ever putting anything on paper. When you are satisfied with what you see on the screen, the word processing program will allow you to print it out or keep it on file (on the disk) for later use.

There are some computers that are designed solely for word processing, but these are out of the realm of "personal" computers. For your purposes, a 16K RAM computer, with a disk drive or cassette and a printer, will produce most letters or short documents. If you are getting into report writing, articles or editing, consider at least 32K, two disk drives, and a better quality printer. Remember that the software should be your first consideration, and the hardware should be chosen to run the program.

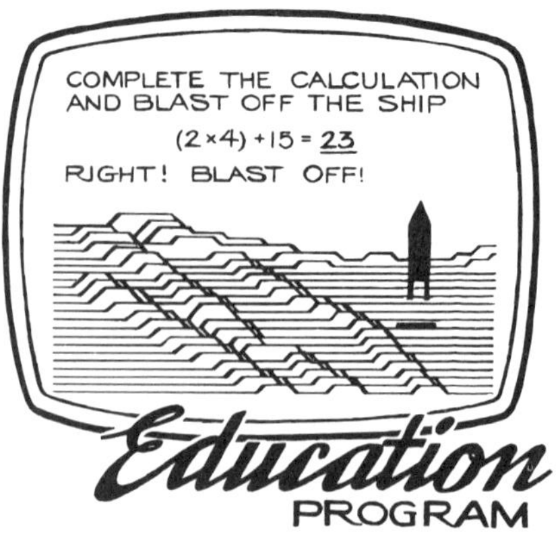

Education

This is an area which I'm sure will see a great growth period in the coming years. Educational programs are designed to help the user master specific skills. There are programs on programming, sentence diagramming (remember that?), vocabulary, mathematics, etc. One reason for the popularity of computers in schools is that kids are not intimidated by them (the story in my Preface is a case in point). Teachers are realizing that computers can assist them in getting students interested and excited about learning. A creative teacher will use a computer as a classroom aid—not as a substitute teacher.

Business

These programs are written to help businesses, small and large, operate more efficiently. Programs have been designed to manage large amounts of data, to do accounts receivable and payable, to write checks, to budget and project budgets, and to help

with inventory. There are programs for household financial tasks like income taxes and balancing checkbooks as well.

One question which is frequently raised when discussing business applications is whether or not a computer is really needed. As we said in Chapter Two, people have lived without computers for a long time and we probably could continue doing so. But in this area particularly, computer assistance has meant increased efficiency. You might not need a 48K system to help you balance your checkbook, but for organizing and maintaining the records of any business the computer can be indispensable.

Games

A look through any computer magazine will demonstrate the popularity of games—both the arcade shoot-'em-up type and the more thought-provoking adventure variety. You can choose from tic-tac-toe to chess, from Mastermind to mystery games, and just about everything you can imagine in between. You can even buy books with programs written out for you to enter into your computer yourself! Software programs for games are available in all computer stores and through mail order—just look at the titles and take your pick! But beware: my family has spent almost as much time playing games with our computer as I have trying to earn a living! If the computer will be part of your livelihood, be sure you're ready to share it before you bring home the games.

Miscellaneous

Here's where I can safely refer to everything else, and there is plenty. Software has been written to allow you to *paint* with your computer, to create poetry, even to write your own music. Remember those people in school who never seemed to be interested in anything but numbers? The computer industry has given them a new outlet, creating programs that can do practically anything. These can be as important as they can be frivolous. It will be worth your time to skim through a few volumes of some popular computer magazines just to get a feel for what's available.

What is most important about software is that it could well be the heart of your decision-making process. In my own case, the software dictated the hardware I would buy. Once I knew what I needed and found that it was available on pre-packaged software, I purchased a computer that the program could run on. If, for example, you know you want Pac-Man and only Pac-Man, and no clone will do, then your choice for hardware is predetermined.

Fortunately, much of the software on the market is compatible with more than one machine, so you still can take other features into consideration. In the next chaper we'll look at some of the features of individual systems so you can begin narrowing your choices.

5 PRODUCT SURVEY

A Do-It-Yourself Systematic Look at Some of the More Popular Computers on the Market Today (which will change by the time you buy this book)

I've put off writing this chapter until the last possible moment. Surveying computer systems is like trying to write about the weather in Maine—by the time you've described it, it has already changed. Today's computer market is extremely volatile. New systems are being introduced, the technology continues to improve, prices fluctuate, and everyone keeps waiting for the Japanese to flood the stores with new products. By the time John Muir Publications gets my manuscript turned into an attractive book for you, who knows what will be on the market?

In order to discuss what is around right now as well as what may be there by the time you read this, I will now present the first-ever do-it-yourself guide to surveying computer products. The first part of the guide is a brief description of a few of the more popular personal computer systems available in the summer of 1983. Almost all the products listed are fairly readily available, have ample service support, and can be purchased for between $100 and $4,000 (the latter including disk drives, monitor, and printer).

Some charts follow which summarize this information as well as enable you to add or change information as changes in the marketplace happen. Finally, we will take a quick look at what is in store for future computer systems.

SOME POPULAR SYSTEMS

Apple IIe

The Apple IIe is the recent successor to the extremely popular *Apple II Plus*. The Apple people say the "e" is for "enhanced," and like its predecessor, the IIe's versatility is well suited to the enormous amount of software available for it. It comes with 64K of RAM, 12K of ROM, and upper and lower case. Its 40-character-by-24-line display can be modified to show 80 columns (characters across), in either monochrome or color. Other enhancements include more arrow keys (for cursor control), and fewer components inside. An RF modulator can be used to connect the computer to your home TV set, and programs can be run either on cassette tape or disk drives. The Apple speaks BASIC, as well as many other languages such as FORTH, LOGO, LISP PASCAL, and FORTRAN.

One great advantage of the Apple is that it has expansion slots which can help you adapt it for almost any use. For example, the Apple can accept an interface card that will let it run CP/M-based programs, even though CP/M is not its native operating system. Other options include sound synthesizers, light pens, "graphics utilities," separate numeric keypad, and many others. Indeed, one advantage Apple has over many other computers is the tremendous amount of hardware and software options available through their own company as well as private vendors. Uses include business and education as well as home applications.

Atari

Atari has capitalized on its fame as a video games leader with its *Atari 400* computer. It has a touch-sensitive (membrane) keyboard for entering information, and can communicate in BASIC, PILOT, FORTH, and other languages. The Atari 400 may be used with its RF modulator as a home and educational computer with some of the most popular video games available. You can buy plug-in pre-programmed cartridges which will run games and application programs in full color on your TV set.

The *Atari 800* would be more suitable if you have more advanced applications in mind, since it is expandable up to 48K of RAM. The 800 in its standard form is basically the same as the 400, except that it has a full stroke typewriter style keyboard instead of the flat membrane keyboard of the 400. Both machines can accept peripherals such as cassette tape storage, printers and game controllers (either "paddles" or "joysticks"). Both Ataris will display 40 characters across by 24 lines and both can be used with a modem. Software and hardware options for the Atari continue to grow as the computers gain acceptance as more than games-players.

There is now a more sophisticated version of the 800, the *1200 XL* (sounds like something you should be able to drive away in). Besides the many attractions of the 800, the 1200 XL comes with 64K RAM and a greater capacity for programming different languages. It is fully compatible with all the Atari peripherals and most of the software available for the 800. Atari has announced plans for the 600XL, 800XL, 1400XL and 1400XLD computers. Assuming (any of) this happens, you will need to see which machine might best suit your needs.

Commodore

If you've ever wondered what Captain Kirk of the Starship Enterprise does in his time off, take a look at the advertisements for the *Commodore VIC-20*. There he is, telling us about Commodore's low-cost home computer designed for use with your TV set. It has a full-size typewriter style keyboard with expandable RAM up to 32K, or up to 43K of ROM. The VIC-20 can display 23 lines of 22 characters across in sixteen (count 'em!) colors. It will show upper and lower case and can be programmed in BASIC or VIGIL. Peripherals available include a single disk drive, modem, paddles, light pen, and printer.

If you like the sound of the VIC-20, take a look at the *Commodore 64*, billed as the "people's computer." The 64 is more than just an upgrade of the VIC-20. It has all the power and many or more of the capabilities of computers selling for twice the price. As its name implies, the Commodore 64 comes with 64K of RAM, plus 20K of ROM. It uses a full-stroke keyboard with eight programmable function keys. The 25-line by 40-column display can be presented in 16 colors with high-resolution graphics. All this, plus the Commodore 64 offers a three-voice music option which can turn your computer into a one-person band.

The 64 can be hooked into the standard Commodore VIC peripherals, including modem, printer, monitor, and disk drives. With the addition of its promised Z80 card, it will run CP/M programs as well. Software can be run with plug-in packages or on cassette or disk, with a fairly good variety now available. Does this all sound too good to be true? Check it out yourself, and see what the Commodore 64 might do for you.

Commodore has also been responsible for the "pets" you may have seen in your local schools lately. The *Commodore PET* (Personal Electronic Transactor) is a multi-purpose machine which uses a full-stroke keyboard with a built-in numeric keypad. It has up to 32K of RAM and will display 40 characters by 25 lines on the 9" monitor which is included (integrated) with the system. The PET comes with the IEEE-488 interface and can converse in BASIC, FORTH, and other languages. All standard Commodore peripherals can be used to expand the PET system. Keep in mind that the Commodore PET and its big brother—the Commodore SuperPET—were designed for educational and business uses. Arcade-type games and color are not readily available. Nonetheless, the PETs are extrememly popular and boast vast amounts of available software.

Epson HX-20

Epson modestly claims to have "sold more printers to this planet than anybody." Now they claim to have a product that will "stand America on its ear." Actually, you can stand the *Epson HX-20* on your ear, since it weighs only four pounds. And it's small enough so that an actual-size picture can fit in a standard magazine display ad. In this tiny package is a computer, cassette drive, monitor and printer! The HX-20 comes with 16K of RAM and 32K of ROM, but can be expanded to 32K of RAM and 64K of ROM. It has a full-stroke keyboard with upper and lower case, ten programmable function keys, and interfaces for cassettes and cartridge programs as well as the standard RS-232C. There's even a floppy disk drive option if more storage is needed.

When the HX-20 arrived in late 1982, I hesitated to include it here—wanting first to see if it became popular. In its first month Epson shipped over 7,500 units of its new computer and projections for future sales remain high. For those who want a little of everything in one small package, the HX-20 could be the answer.

IBM

Think what you will about giant conglomerates, IBM has been a leader in the computer field from its very beginnings. While most of its computers are designed for large businesses and institutions, the cleverly named *IBM Personal Computer* is touted for home, business and educational use. It features 16K to 256K of RAM, a full-stroke typewriter-style keyboard, built-in numeric pad, and upper and lower case letters on its 80-character by 25-line screen. Display can be in monochrome or full color. The IBM uses BASIC, PASCAL, FORTRAN, and other languages. It comes with the RS-232C interface, and can be expanded to accept up to two disk drives, modem, printer, and high resolution (very clear) graphics. Other accessories such as light pen and joystick can also be added.

When I wrote the first draft of this book, I suggested that the one drawback of the IBM-PC was its lack of software and peripheral hardware. What a difference a few months can make! As sales of the PC skyrocketed, software publishers got their wares on the shelves very quickly. You should have no problem finding the programs you need.

Look for a new product from IBM — code named "Peanut" — sometime soon. Rumors of its arrival have already shaken the computer world. No doubt the Peanut, along with the PC, will share in setting the "industry standard."

COLECO

It seems a bit strange that in the garden of Eden of the computer world it took Adam so long to arrive. Adam, in case you haven't heard, is Coleco's entry into the home computer market. Of course, you must know this, because the Adam has received as much press — from the Wall Street Journal to this book — as the IBM Peanut! The only problem seems to be that Coleco had some last minute production problems, so the real Adam may look a little different from this description.

The way I hear it, though, the Adam will come with everything you need for personal computing except a monitor. What is "everything?" In Coleco's vision, it is a computer with 80K of RAM, a full stroke, 75-key detachable keyboard with programmable function keys, 2 game controllers with number pads, and a 500K data-pack tape drive. The latter does the storage job of a disk drive but uses a tape instead of a disk. Adam's tape drive is said to move at up to 100 inches per second — much faster than other tape systems.

But, that's not all, folks. The Adam will come with a built-in word processing program called Smartwriter. The keyboard has special keys to take advantage of Smartwriter's features. And, to see your work in print, Adam also includes a letter quality printer. It uses a daisy wheel for typing up to ten characters per second.

Adam uses the ever-popular CP/M operating system, giving it access to thousands of programs. Software should become available for the data-pack shortly after Adam's release.

All this is said to be available for less than the cost of an inexpensive letter quality printer. If so, Adam just might live up to its name.

Osborne

Now this really shows you how volatile the computer market is. The Osborne 1 was the low-cost portable computer that started the whole continuing trend towards smaller, more powerful machines. Among other things, it was also the computer that started the "bundled software" approach. Its price included virtually all the software a small business might need. Many will speculate why, but the fact is that the Osborne Computer Corporation declared bankruptcy in September, 1983. We don't know if this will mean the end of the company, but the existence of thousands of their computers means you should know about them. Be aware that on October 11, 1983, Osborne announced that the Xerox Corporation would take over warrantees and servicing of Osborne computers. So if you have or get one, you should be protected. Now, if you are still reading, this is what the Osborne is about...

The machine itself has a full-stroke keyboard with numeric pad and can display upper and lower case characters. With an external 12" monitor (optional) it will display 80 characters by 25 lines, but the integrated 5" screen will only display 54 characters by 24 lines, although it can be scrolled (moved around) to display up to 128 characters by 32 lines. If this display information seems confusing to you, go see the Osborne-1 for a demonstration of its scrolling abilities.

You might be wondering how convenient it would be to look at a five-inch screen with all that scrolling around. Lots of other people wondered the same thing. So in May 1983, the *Osborne Executive* series was announced. The Executive has a bright, new 7" (diagonal) amber screen. The disk drives were upgraded to double density, and there is now 128K to 256K of RAM available. In addition to the CP/M programs already available for the Osborne, the new *Executive 2* will also be able to run programs written for the IBM.

The different rivals in the portable world are Radio Shack (Model 100), Texas Instruments, Non-Linear Systems (Kaypro), Access, Otrona, and Compac. If portability is important to you, be sure to explore this expanding market before you make your final choice.

Radio Shack (TRS-80)

Ahh, where to begin? The Tandy/Radio Shack (TRS) people have a 56-page catalog of TRS-80 computers ranging from their PC-1 pocket computer to the Model 16 business system. Included in the catalog is a full range of computers, printers, disk drives and other peripherals, as well as software for almost any application. Since we don't have space to cover them all, let's look at three of Radio Shack's more popular personal computers: the TRS-80 Color Computer, the TRS-80 Models II and III, and the new Model 100.

The *TRS-80 Color Computer* is designed primarily for home and entertainment applications. It supports a myriad of software which can be run through a cartridge port, tape cassette, or up to four disk drives. The Color Computer has a full-stroke keyboard and comes with 4K RAM standard, but can expand to 32K and will accept programs written in BASIC. As the name implies, full color is available with high resolution graphics on a 32-character by 16-line display of upper case characters. The Color Computer can be hooked up to your home TV, and will accept options such as joysticks, printer, modem, etc.

The *TRS-80 Model II* is an integrated unit which includes full-stroke keyboard, 12" monitor, and optional disk drives. The standard Model II has 4K of RAM, but can be expanded to 48K. There is a built-in printer interface and room for many other options.

The *TRS-80 Model III* can accept programs written in BASIC, COBOL, FORTRAN and other languages. There are over 2,400 available software programs written for this machine.

The trend in the computer industry right now is the production of small, portable, low-cost business computers.

To this end, Radio Shack has released the *TRS-80 Model 100*. This is a three-and-a-half pound machine that can be run either by house current or with batteries. The Model 100 features a full-stroke keyboard with eight programmable function keys, and comes with 8K of RAM (expandable to 32K) and 32K of ROM. Upper and lower case letters can be displayed in eight lines, 40 columns across on the built-in LCD screen. With its built-in modem and programming capabilities, the Model 100 makes an interesting choice for the traveling businessperson.

As with some of the other computers mentioned here the TRS-80s offer enormous choices for software, plus nationwide access to sales and service through Radio Shack stores. Other factors being equal, accessibility to your dealer could be an important factor in choosing your computer. You might find a Radio Shack Computer Center in your neighborhood. These specialized stores offer even greater support of TRS products.

Sinclair

In a class by itself right now is the *Sinclair ZX-81*, which is also marketed as the *Timex/Sinclair 1000*. This is a tiny computer with a membrane (touch sensitive) keyboard which is fully programmable in BASIC. It comes with 1K RAM and can be expanded to 16K with a plug-in module. A cassette tape player can provide extra storage space, if needed. The Timex/Sinclair is designed to be hooked up to your home TV where it will display upper case letters in 32 characters by 24 lines, black and white only. An optional printer is available which can hard-copy most of the characters or graphics symbols produced by the computer. Like the Osborne, the Sinclair's breakthrough is in size and price. This hand-held computer is priced around $50. Though software and hardware are limited, the Sinclair can be very useful for applications in the home, or just for learning about computers.

Texas Instruments

That computer you see under the smiling face of one of my favorite educators, Dr. Bill Cosby, is the *Texas Instruments 99/4A*. This is a very inexpensive machine which will accept plug-in cartridge or disk-driven programs. The 99/4A can be expanded to 52K of RAM and 30K of ROM. Its full-stoke keyboard will produce upper case letters and full color displays. Options include modems, speech devices, disk drives and printers. This is essentially a home and education computer with a limited, although expanding, range of software. It can be programmed in BASIC, PASCAL, PILOT, and the increasingly popular LOGO.

* * * * *

If you read the newspapers or magazines, you know we've only touched the surface of the computer market. Besides the many other manufacturers we have not discussed, some of those we have mentioned also produce other models not included here. For example, Radio Shack makes a hand-held computer as well as a high-capacity business machine. Apple has the Apple III for business uses, Commodore has a few other models, as do other makers. But now you have an overview of some of the more popular machines, and you can go out and compare other computers to these.

THE DO-IT-YOURSELF CHART, AS PROMISED

Here's a chart you can use to comparison-shop the different computers, or to revise information as it changes. It's pretty straightforward, but let's go over the ground rules. Remember, comparing a 4K computer to a 64K computer is much akin to comparing apples to oranges. The left-hand side of the chart allows you to fill in the various standard and

THE DO-IT-YOURSELF COMPUTER COMPARISON AND PRICE CHART

FEATURES	**Computer:** **Dealer:**	**Computer:** **Dealer:**	**Computer:** **Dealer:**	**Computer:** **Dealer:**
Basic Price				
Memory Size Add'l RAM? Add'l ROM? Extra Cost:				

Display (Output) Type of monitor: Monitor price: Display size: Color capacity? Graphics? Lower case? Sound? Extra costs:				
Keyboard Membrane type? Full stroke? Numeric pad? Extra costs:				

Storage Cassette? Price: One disk drive? Price: Two disk drives? Price:				
Printer Type? Price:				
Interfaces Type? Price: Type? Price:				

Other Peripherals (modem, etc.) Type? Price: Type? Price:				
Software Name? Price: Name? Price: Name? Price:				

Services Warranty Repair Extra costs:				
Miscellaneous Extra goodies: Extra costs:				
TOTAL SYSTEM COST:				

optional features you come across in your shopping or ad-reading. Use the corresponding boxes to pencil in whatever information you need. There's room across the top to fill in names of your favorite computers and the dealers. If you need more room, I've provided extra blank charts at the back of the book. As you complete the chart you can see how the computers compare with each other in features, then in prices-per-feature. This latter part will come in handy when we get to Chapter Seven: *Dollars and Dealing*.

A QUICK LOOK AT THE FUTURE

I started this chapter with a statement about the weather in Maine. In fairness, I'll end with an analogy about the position of the San Andreas Fault: it, like the computer market, can shift at any moment.

One problem with discussing the future of the computer market is that much of the future is already here—at least in experimental form. Another problem is that the technology itself is creating its own future, so it's hard for mere mortals to keep up.

Given these disclaimers, let's look at how the market *might* change, and how this might affect your purchase of a computer.

Probably the greatest trend at the moment is one that has been going on for awhile already. Remember the names of the early computers—names like *Eniac* and *Univac*? These were monstrous units that took up whole rooms with blinking lights and whirring tape reels. You still see them in old movies late at night. Microcomputers today are as potent as the old giants, and the size is getting smaller and smaller. The trend seems to be toward the portable integrated system, like the Kaypro and Otrona. Look for more of these in the near future.

Another promising trend, and one that is already being test marketed, is the home television information system known as *videotex*. Videotex is basically a way of communicating with other computer banks using your home computer and your TV or telephone. It is an *interactive* system, meaning you can receive as well as send information. Think of what this might mean to you! Tired of shopping? How about using your videotex system to show you a department store catalog on the screen of your TV.

Once you decide what you want, you can send in your order—over the same videotex lines. Airline tickets can be ordered this way, and your whole banking experience can be conducted from your living room sofa. Science fiction? No—*it's already here!* In fact, the Radio Shack TRS-80 catalog devotes two of its 56 pages to videotex terminals. The videotex revolution is part of the growing trend of shopping and working at home.

Teletext is a related service which operates in similar fashion to videotex. Teletext uses television airwaves or cable lines to transmit information as requested by the user. This might include any or all of the examples we mentioned in the videotex paragraph above. The big difference, though, is that you can't talk back with teletext—you can only receive information.

Watch for the giants of the television and telephone industries to get involved in videotex and teletext. AT&T is already involved, along with other such notables as CBS, Dow Jones, *The New York Times*, CompuServ, The Source, TIME Inc., Cox Cable Co., *Reader's Digest*, etc. If it all happens as predicted, you might want to make sure your computer can help you get involved.

Electronic mail is another trend area you might take a look

at. This is a way of sending your message from point A to point B over a data link-up such as a central data bank or a telephone line (called *electronic telephony,* believe it or not).

As quickly as the changes happen in the hardware, the software will be right behind. New programs are on the market literally every day. Another trend is toward "emulator" cards. These will enable computers to think like other computers. For example, right now the Commodore machines cannot use programs written for Apple machines. With an emulator, the Commodore can be fooled into thinking it is an Apple, and vice-versa (see, they're not so smart . . . or are they?). Thus, if you really like the hardware of one computer, but are afraid you won't find enough available software, one of the new emulators might be your solution.

Do you need a computer just to process all this? Not really. But as we will discuss again later, there is always a question of whether to buy now or to wait until the market changes again. Although there is no firm answer to this question, remember that the computer you choose can never do less than it did the day you bought it. So if it meets your needs now, it may easily be worth the investment. Your task is to identify your needs for today and the future and find the software and hardware to meet those needs. Chapter Six will help. Read on.

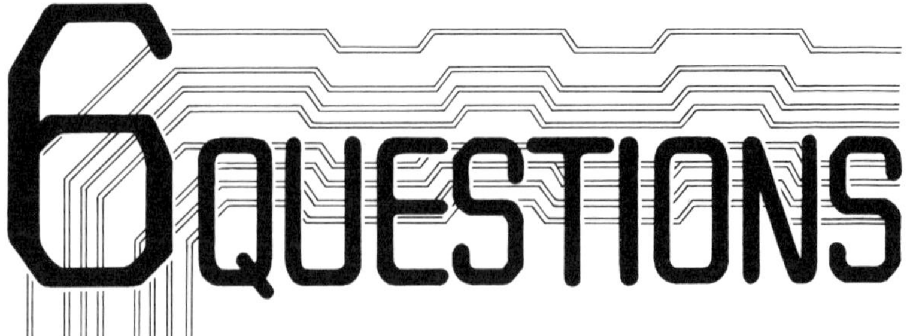

6 QUESTIONS

What to Ask Yourself and the Dealer

For the most part, I've been doing the larger share of the work up to this point. Sure, you've had to learn a lot, but it's been fun, hasn't it? Meanwhile, I've been staying up late every night putting all this information together for you. But now the time has come for you to take action on your own. This chapter is on questions you should ask, and I can't answer them for you. Like making the final decision, this is something only you can do. But perhaps you'd like a little guidance? This might help:

A Short Quiz on Deciding What You Need in a Personal Computer

1) Answer yes or no:
   Do you need a computer? _____
2) Answer yes or no:
   Do you want a computer? _____

If *either* of the questions above was answered "yes," you may continue. If both questions were answered "no," please pass this book along to a good friend.

3) If you had to narrow down all the things you'd like the computer to do, what would be the number one priority? (*e.g.*: I'd like it to assist me in writing a book about computers.)

____

____

____

4) In question 3 you listed the primary thing you'd like the computer to accomplish. Now let's break that down into specific parts. List at least three components of the task mentioned above. (*e.g.*: I need the ability to edit on screen; I need upper and lower case letters; I need mailing labels, etc.)

a) ______________________________

____

b) ______________________________

____

c) ______________________________

____

d) ______________________________

____

e) ______________________________

____

5) Now list, in order of rank, the other important tasks you have in mind for the computer. (*e.g.*: Data Base management, educational programming, household budgeting, games.)

a) ______________________________

b) ______________________________

c) ______________________________

d) ______________________________

6) From the Yellow Pages, under "Computer Sales" or something similar, find the names of at least five different computers. List them and the names and addresses of stores where they can be seen.

a) ______________________________

____

b) ______________________________

____

c) ______________________________

____

d) ______________________________

____

e) ______________________________

____

f) ______________________________

____

End Of Quiz

INFORMATION YOU WANT

It's almost time to go out into the computer world again—although this time you know what to expect and you're prepared! Let's just take a few more minutes to review some of the information you should try to get while you are out there on the road:

A. Software

1. Discuss with the salesperson the specific applications you've outlined above. Ask if there is any software available which will help meet your needs, or if you will have to use custom-designed programs.

2. Ask to see a display of software available for the machines sold in the store. Give yourself some time to scan the shelves, just as you might in a bookstore. Do the titles look interesting? Will some of the software programs fill your needs? Ask about them. See which programs are compatible with which machines in the store.

3. Ask for a demonstration of the software that looked interesting. Does it do what you want it to do? Does it look difficult? Read through the manual (called "documentation," remember?). Can you get the gist of it, or is it too technical? Will the salesperson provide training for software use?

B. Computer

1. Is the computer capable of performing the tasks or applications you listed above? Better still, will it handle the packaged software you've chosen? If not, can it be programmed to do what you need?

2. Does the computer have the ability to change if your needs change? Can you add to its memory? Will it handle color graphics if you need them? Can it display video games? Is there software available now for these applications—in case you want to use them later?

3. Can the computer display 80 columns (characters across) if you need it? If not, can the present line length be extended? Can it display upper and lower case letters? If not, is there a way to get these to your printer?

4. Ask the dealer to demonstrate the computer doing what you listed as your number one priority. See if you can make some entries and get some information out of the machine. Does it have a good "feel?" Can you adapt to its individual

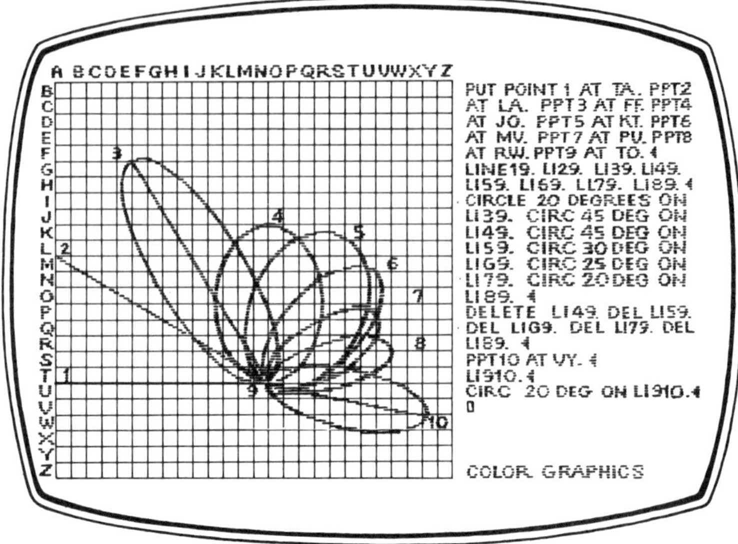

quirks? Or, would you rather see a machine with a different design or features?

C. Disk Drives

1. In many cases disk drives will be built-in (integrated) with the computer system (Osborne and TRS-80 Model III, for instance). How much data can be stored on each drive? Which DOS does it use? Can dual sided disks be used? Can storage capacity be expanded if you need more? Are interfaces available now? Are they expensive? Will there be any limitation on the types of diskettes you can use?

D. Printer

1. Ask to see samples of the typefaces available with the different printers. Be sure you get the combination that best suits you. Do you need letter quality with formed characters, or can you use a less expensive dot matrix printer?

2. How noisy is the machine? Listen to it. Will it disturb your family at 11 pm?

3. What kind(s) of paper can be used? Can you insert single sheets?

4. How difficult is it to change the ribbon cartridge? How often will it have to be replaced? Is there any other regular maintenance you will have to do to the printer?

E. Monitor

1. Do you need color graphics? If not, do you need high-resolution? Can you make out the printing on the screen clearly as you see it demonstrated? Are the adjustments accessible? Are any special interfaces needed, or can it be plugged directly into the computer?

F. Dealer

What kind of assistance can the dealer provide? Try to get answers to the following questions:

1. How long will the purchase stay under warranty? If you have to bring your computer in for repair, what arrangements are made for a loaner system?

2. Is there an in-house service person? Which items can they repair in the store and which ones have to be sent out?

3. How long has the store been in business? Can the owner or manager give you names of satisfied customers? Will she or he supply the name of someone who had a defective computer and needed service?

4. Perhaps most importantly, will the dealer give *you* support? Can you get the training you need? Do the people in the store know how to run the computers and the compatible software? Does everyone seem to know what they're talking about?

* * * * *

This chapter has been about getting you prepared for your next jaunt to the computer store. If you've done your homework, you should have:

- a list of reasons for wanting a computer.
- some books or magazines which have gotten you acquainted with the computer world.
- a vocabulary of Computerese.
- some notion about how a computer and its related peripherals work.
- basic knowledge about the availability of software.
- familiarity with the variety of machines on the market.
- a list of the applications you have in mind for your computer.
- a slew of questions to ask at the computer store.
- your Yellow Pages listing of the dealers in your neighborhood.

That last item should be on top of the pile because you are now ready to shop around. But remember—don't buy anything just yet. Collect information about the many different components available to you. With all of your new knowledge about computers, you should be able to get enough data together after a few trips to the stores in your area to make an informed, intelligent decision.

Take your lists of applications and questions along, and take a clipboard with scratch paper. Collect lots of information and write everything down. The clipboard will help you with the brochures and flyers you'll be handed at every stop. When you get back, we'll start our final discussion—on making the deal.

7 DOLLARS AND DEALING

The main focus of this book has been to help you make an intelligent decision about buying a personal computer. No products have been endorsed, and none have been rejected. All the computers, peripherals and software you have seen have their advantages and their disadvantages. Maybe some of the systems meet your needs perfectly while others do not. If you're like me, you have found that there are a number of systems which will work for you. This makes your choice a little more difficult, but far from impossible.

Many factors, some more important than others, should help guide you in your final buying decision. We discussed most of these in Chapter Six. Dealer support should be near the top of the list. If you felt more comfortable in one store than in any of the others, and if that dealer is reputable and stable and sells the wares that'll do your job, you should probably buy your system there. Service contracts, warranties, training, and other non-money components should all enter into your decision.

This is not to say that money is a secondary factor. As of this writing, personal computers are selling from $49.95 to well over $10,000 for a completely configured system. Prices seem to be going down for the hardware, but up for the software, so waiting to buy might not necessarily save you any money.

On the other hand, new systems are being introduced constantly. If you haven't found anything to your liking yet, you might want to wait a little while for the next generations of computers and peripherals to be released. Beware of promises, though. If you are hesitant to buy a computer because it has a given limitation (line length is too short), but the dealer says the manufacturer is about to release an "upgrade," you should wait for the upgrade to appear before buying. The upgrades never seem to arrive when they're supposed to, leaving you waiting with your limited-function machine.

Another pricing consideration has to do with mail-order sales. All the computer magazines have pages of advertisements from companies ready to sell you a computer system through the mail. Usually their prices are much lower than the dealer's. However, when you add in the shipping costs, the difference might not be that great. You need to consider the service and support element at this point. If, like me, you'll be needing help getting started with your computer, you might be better off paying the extra few dollars to assure your local dealer's assistance. Asking for advice or help with a system bought from someone else is like going into a restaurant with your own food—they might not throw you out, but you could wait around a long time for service. If, on the other hand, you don't think you will need a local dealer's support, take a closer look at mail order—you'll undoubtedly save some money.

Another consideration is whether or not to get more than you really need right now. This is a hard one to answer. Project into the future, with some sober accuracy, if you can. If you don't see your needs changing significantly in three to five years, there is no need to get an omnipotent system. If growth is in the picture, however, you should consider a system that will grow with you.

Given all this, let's get down to the "bottom line." How much will all this cost you? It helped me to use a chart for comparing costs at different stores. The chart in Chapter Five helped you to compare different systems with similar capabilities. We've included extra blank charts at the back of the book, if you need them. If you didn't do it back then, your next step should be to pull out this chart and get the information you need. If you already did this in Chapter Five, retrieve your copies so you can review the actual costs from different shops.

If you've done your shopping well you should be able to complete the entire chart. If there are some gaps, call the stores and get quotes over the phone. When you get to the bottom of the chart, add up the columns for your system prices. This might eliminate some of the dealers immediately.

When I was searching, I set a maximum dollar amount for myself. Anything over that could not be considered further. You should do the same—it'll help you figure out what you can and cannot afford, and keep you honest with yourself. Remember, though, the list price might not be the final offer. Most dealers are willing to negotiate with you. These negotiations might revolve around actual dollars, increased service, a few "goodies" thrown in (software, paper, a box of disks, etc.), or something else you might need to sweeten the deal. This is where you need to be your most assertive. Tell the dealer what you need and what you are willing to pay. Negotiate firmly and you will probably save yourself some money!

Once you have completed your chart(s) and figured out what you are willing to negotiate for, make a return trip to the dealers. I suggest you discuss your situation honestly with each of them: tell them that you are looking at a few different systems, that they all look attractive to you, and that you are down to dollars and cents. Ask the dealer for his best possible bid. If you will be paying in cash or with a credit card, be sure the dealer knows this. If you will need financing, you might not want to discuss this until the final price is quoted.

When all the quotes are in, my job with you is completed. You're on your own to make your decision. Consider everything you've read about in this book. Remember that cheapest isn't always best, but neither is most expensive. Your decision should be based on an understanding of your needs. A savings of $250 on a computer that doesn't fill your needs is no saving at all. Paying a little more for peace of mind will be worth it in the long run.

There is one other thing you should do, if you haven't already. Call everyone you know who owns a computer. Ask their advice. If they bought locally, ask about the local stores. Listen to their suggestions and recommendations, and filter all this through with your own thoughts. Sleep on it, spend the next day running it through your mind again, and, if your decision to buy still feels right, do it!

Computers Give You More Time to Daydream

Do-It-Yourself
Computer Comparison
&
Price Chart

THE DO-IT-YOURSELF COMPUTER COMPARISON AND PRICE CHART

FEATURES	**Computer:** **Dealer:**	**Computer:** **Dealer:**	**Computer:** **Dealer:**	**Computer:** **Dealer:**
Basic Price				
Memory Size Add'l RAM? Add'l ROM? Extra Cost:				

Display (Output) Type of monitor: Monitor price: Display size: Color capacity? Graphics? Lower case? Sound? Extra costs:				
Keyboard Membrane type? Full stroke? Numeric pad? Extra costs:				

Storage Cassette? Price: One disk drive? Price: Two disk drives? Price:				
Printer Type? Price:				
Interfaces Type? Price: Type? Price:				

Other Peripherals (modem, etc.) Type? Price: Type? Price:				
Software Name? Price: Name? Price: Name? Price:				

Services				
Warranty				
Repair				
Extra costs:				
Miscellaneous				
Extra goodies:				
Extra costs:				
TOTAL SYSTEM COST:				

More Useful & Entertaining Books from John Muir Publications

How to Keep Your Honda Car Alive
by Fred Cisin & Jack Parvin (14.00)

How to Keep Your VW Rabbit Alive
by Richard Sealey (15.00)

How to Keep Your Volkswagen Alive
by John Muir (12.50)

Flea Market America: A Bargain Hunter's Guide
by Cree McCree (8.50)

The People's Guide to Mexico
(Revised) by Carl Franz (10.50)

The People's Guide to Camping in Mexico
by Carl Franz (10.00)

The On and Off the Road Cookbook
by Carl Franz and Lorena Havens (8.50)

A Guide to Midwifery: Heart and Hands
by Elizabeth Davis (9.00)

A Guide to Dying at Home
by Deborah Duda (7.50)

The Art of Running
by Michael Schreiber (9.00)

The Food and Heat Producing Solar Greenhouse
(Revised) by Bill Yanda & Rick Fisher (8.00)

The Bountiful Solar Greenhouse
by Shane Smith (8.00)

The Guitar Owner's Manual
by Will Martin (6.95)

Word Processing and Beyond
by Fred Stern (9.00)

Postage: Add $1 for postage and handling

ORDER BLANKS

JOHN MUIR PUBLICATIONS
P.O. Box 613 SANTA FE, NM 87504-0613

Enclosed is $__________ for _____ copies of *Computer-Ease* @ $6.95 each plus $1 postage & handling. Please send to:

NAME ______________________________

ADDRESS ______________________________

CITY ______________________________

STATE ______________ ZIP ______________

(Allow 3 weeks for delivery)

11-83

JOHN MUIR PUBLICATIONS
P.O. Box 613 SANTA FE, NM 87504-0613

Enclosed is $__________ for _____ copies of *Computer-Ease* @ $6.95 each plus $1 postage & handling. Please send to:

NAME ______________________________

ADDRESS ______________________________

CITY ______________________________

STATE ______________ ZIP ______________

(Allow 3 weeks for delivery)

11-83